Big and Little

A ZEBRA BOOK

By John Satchwell

Illustrated by Katy Sleight

PUBLISHED BY

WALKER BOOKS

LONDON

Today the monster
is going on holiday.

tight

loose

long

short

big

little

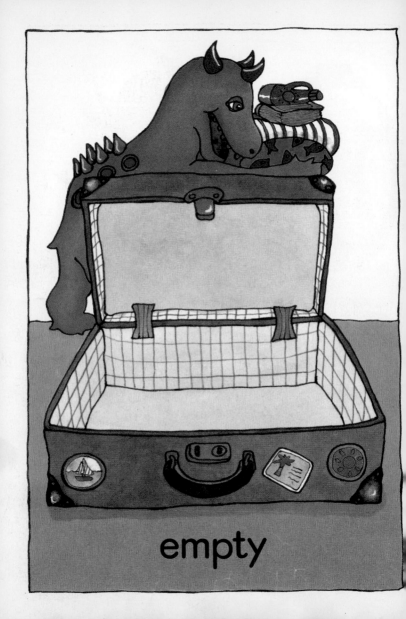

empty

full

top

bottom

down

wet

dry

fast

slow

hard

soft

thick

thin

awake

asleep